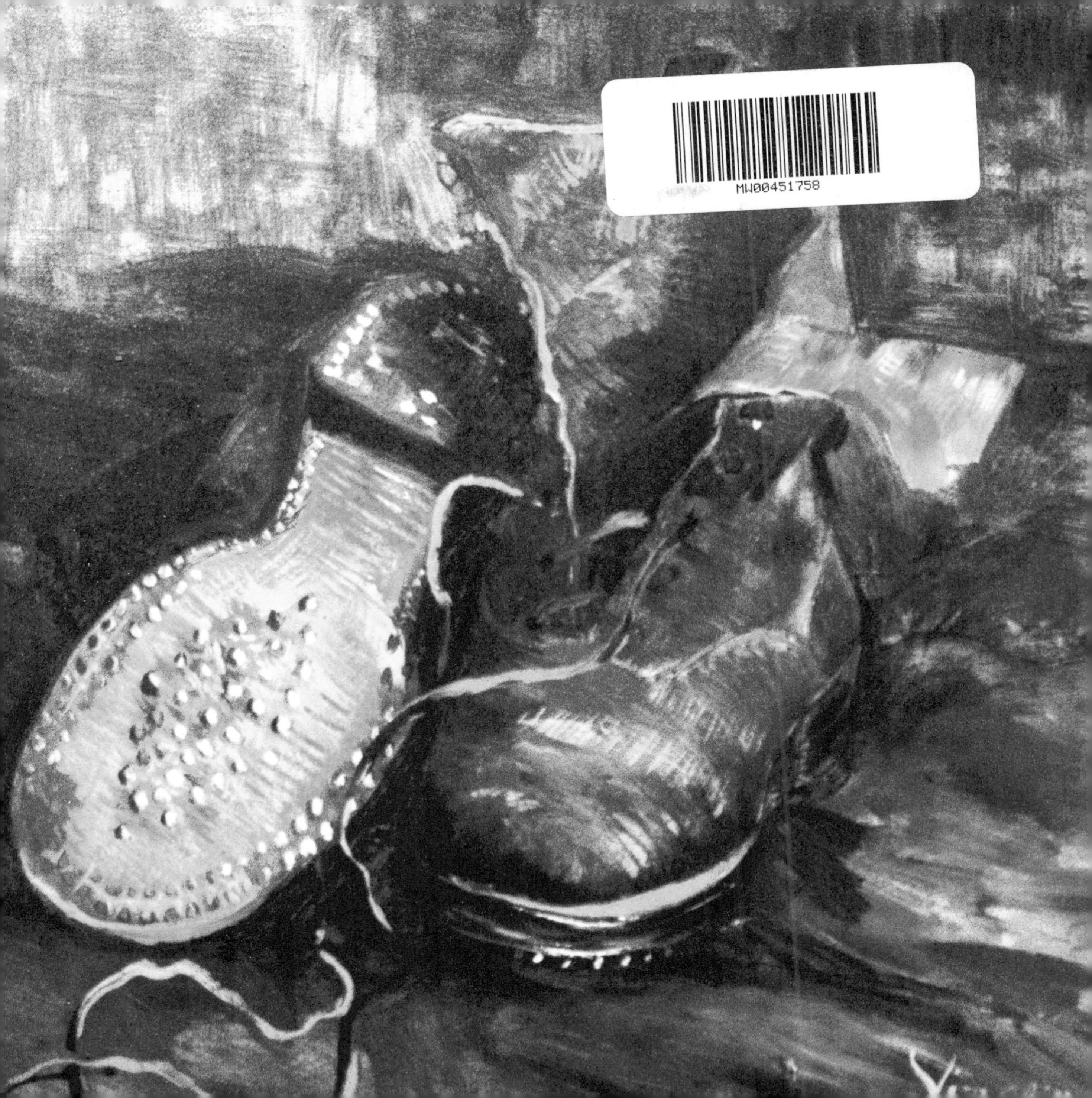

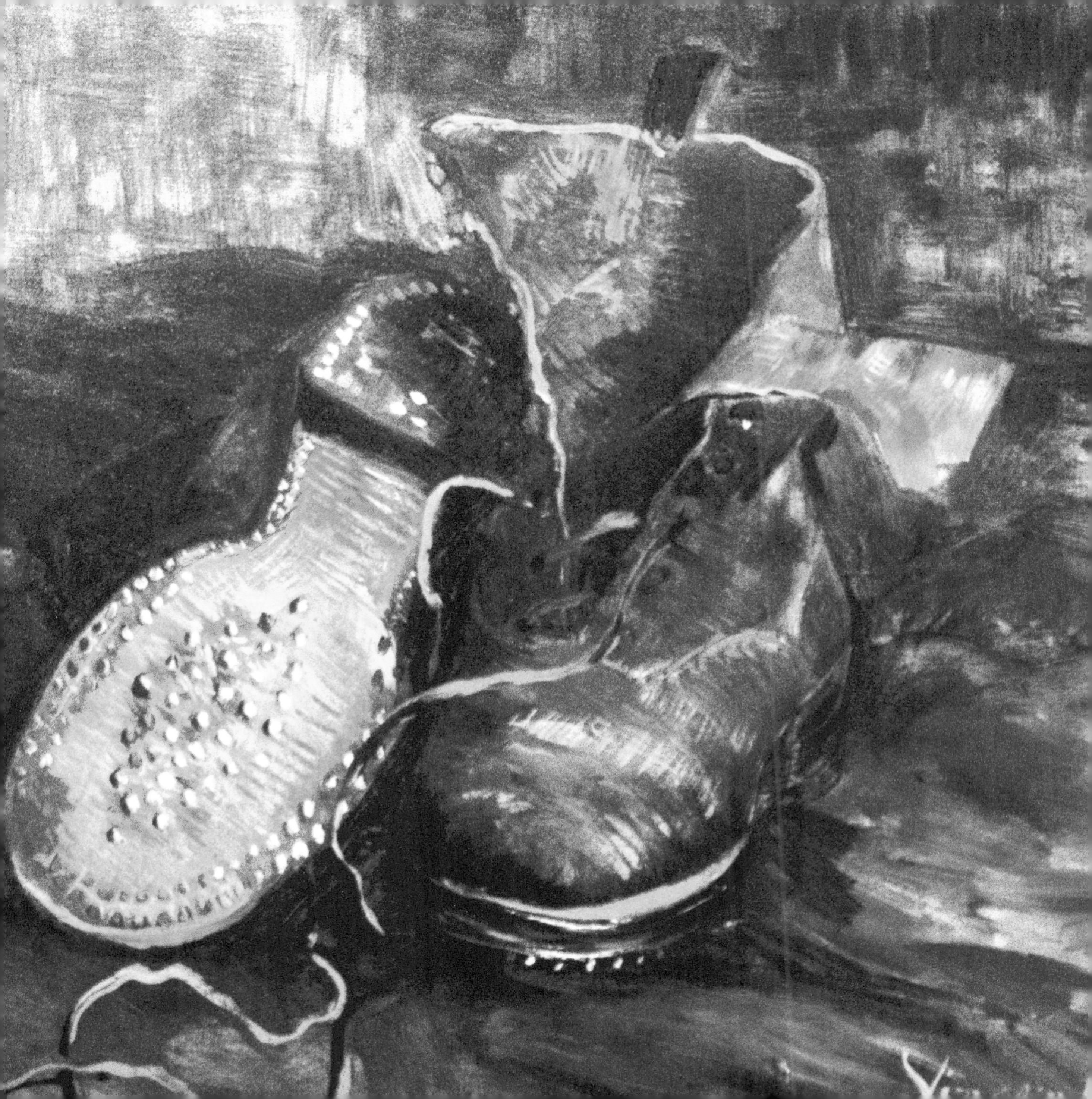

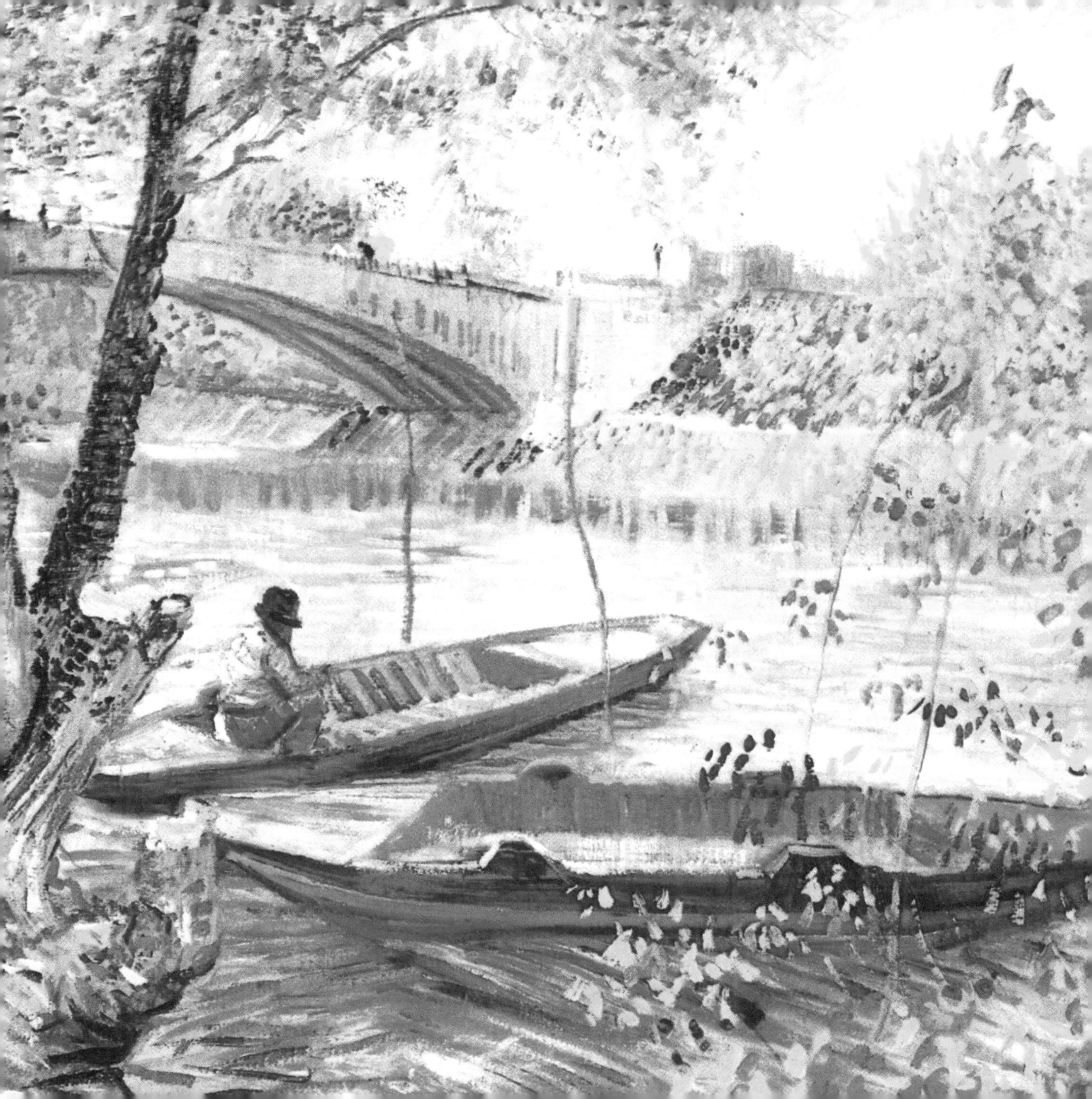

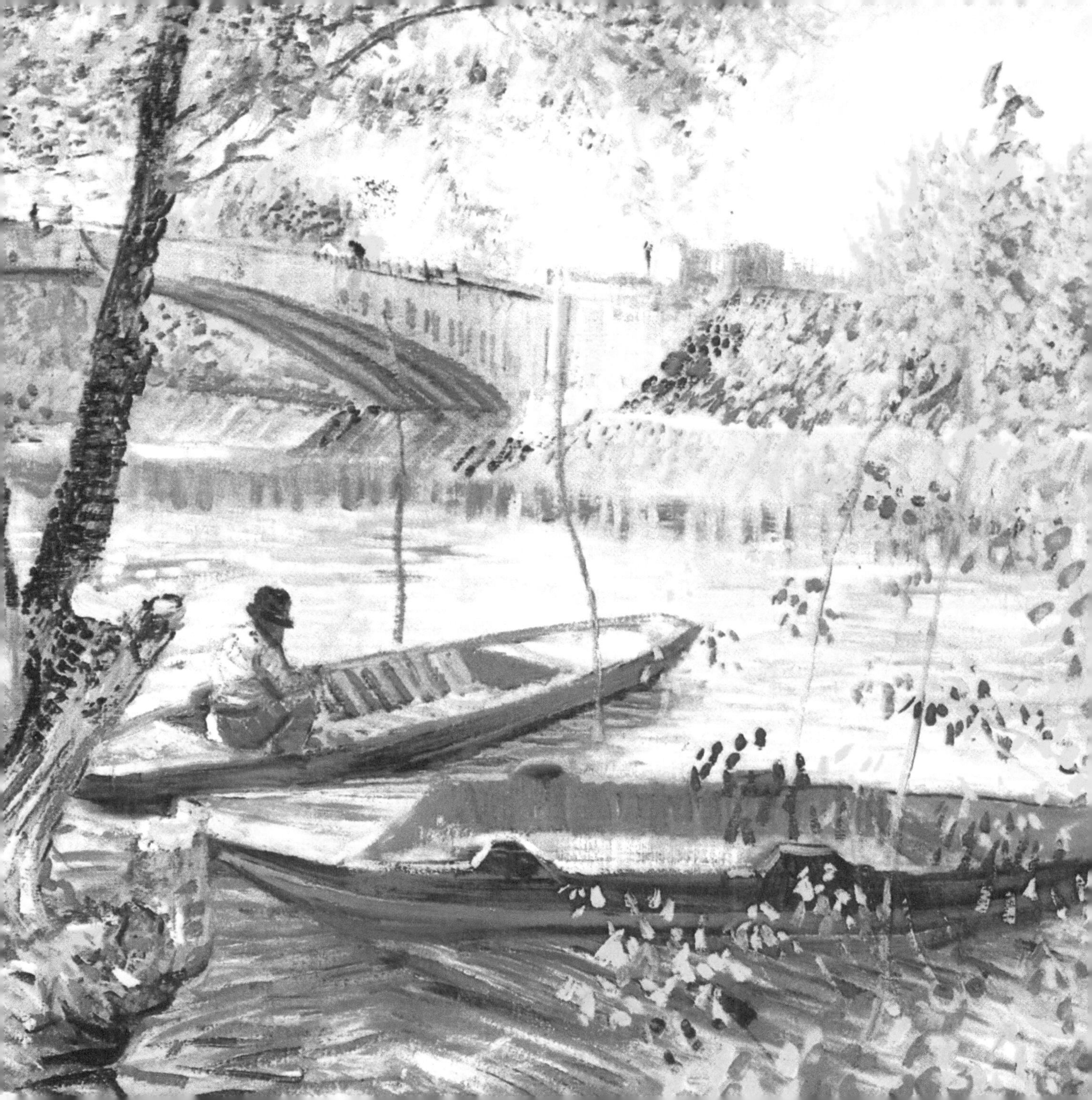

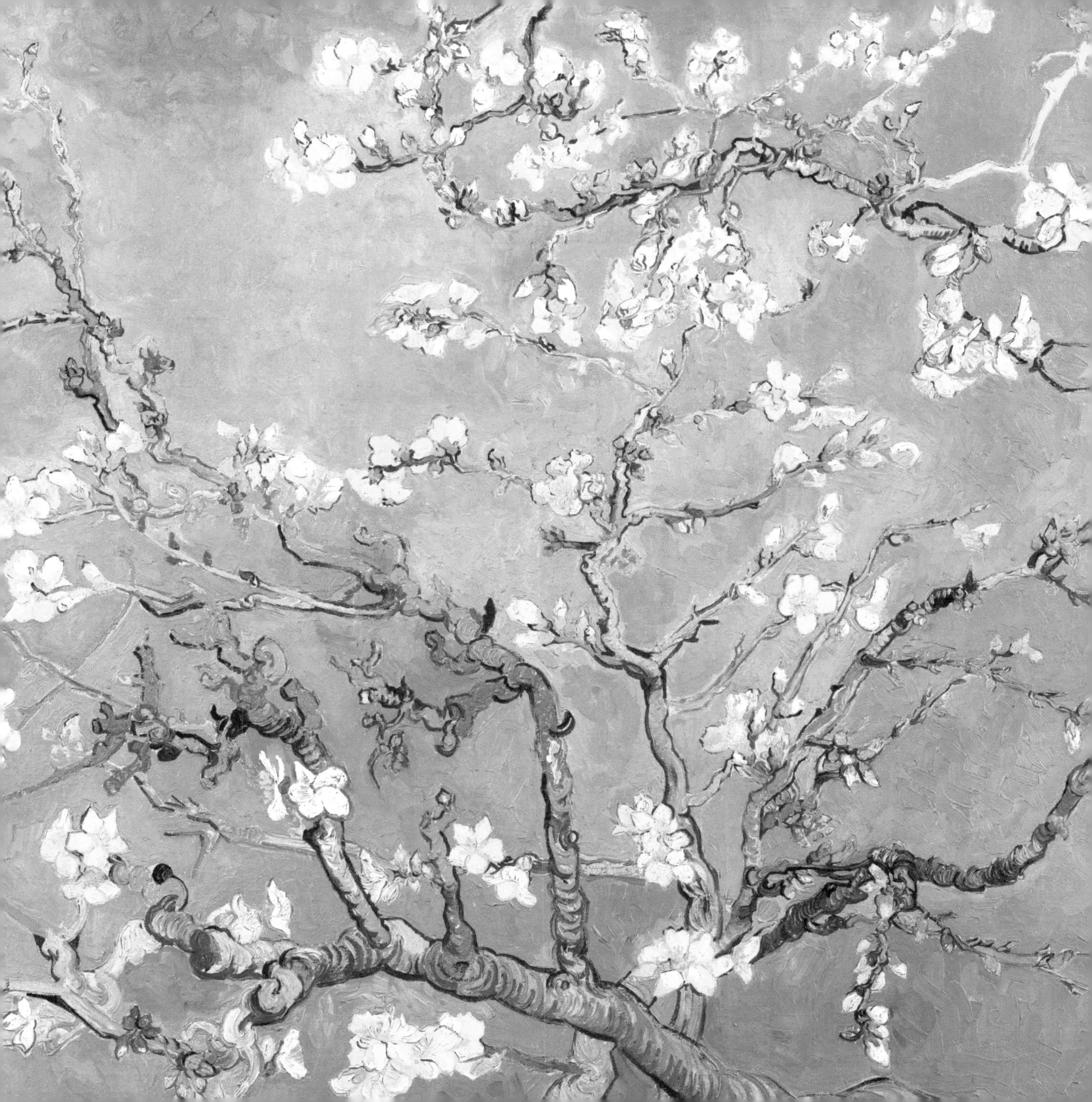

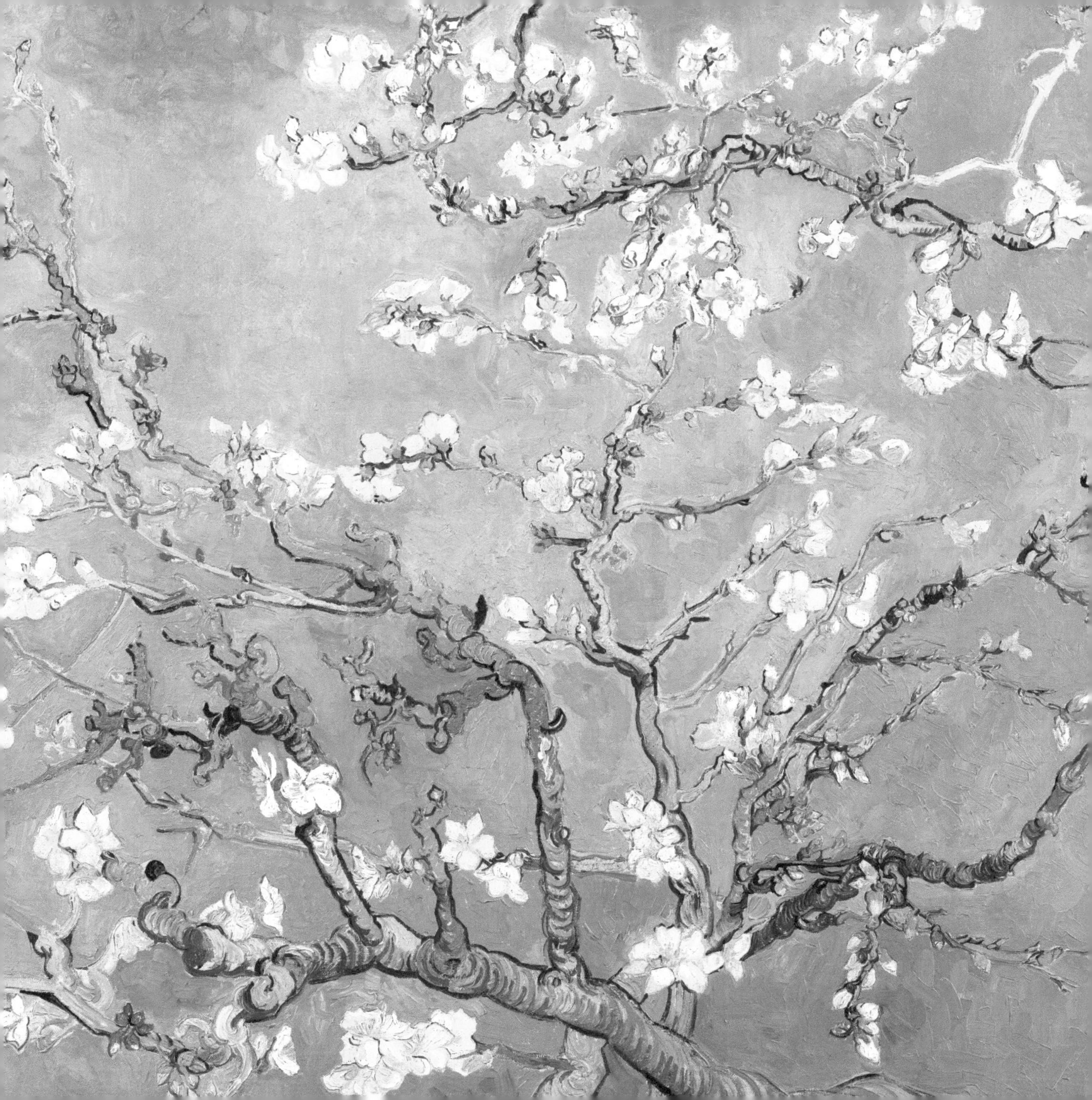

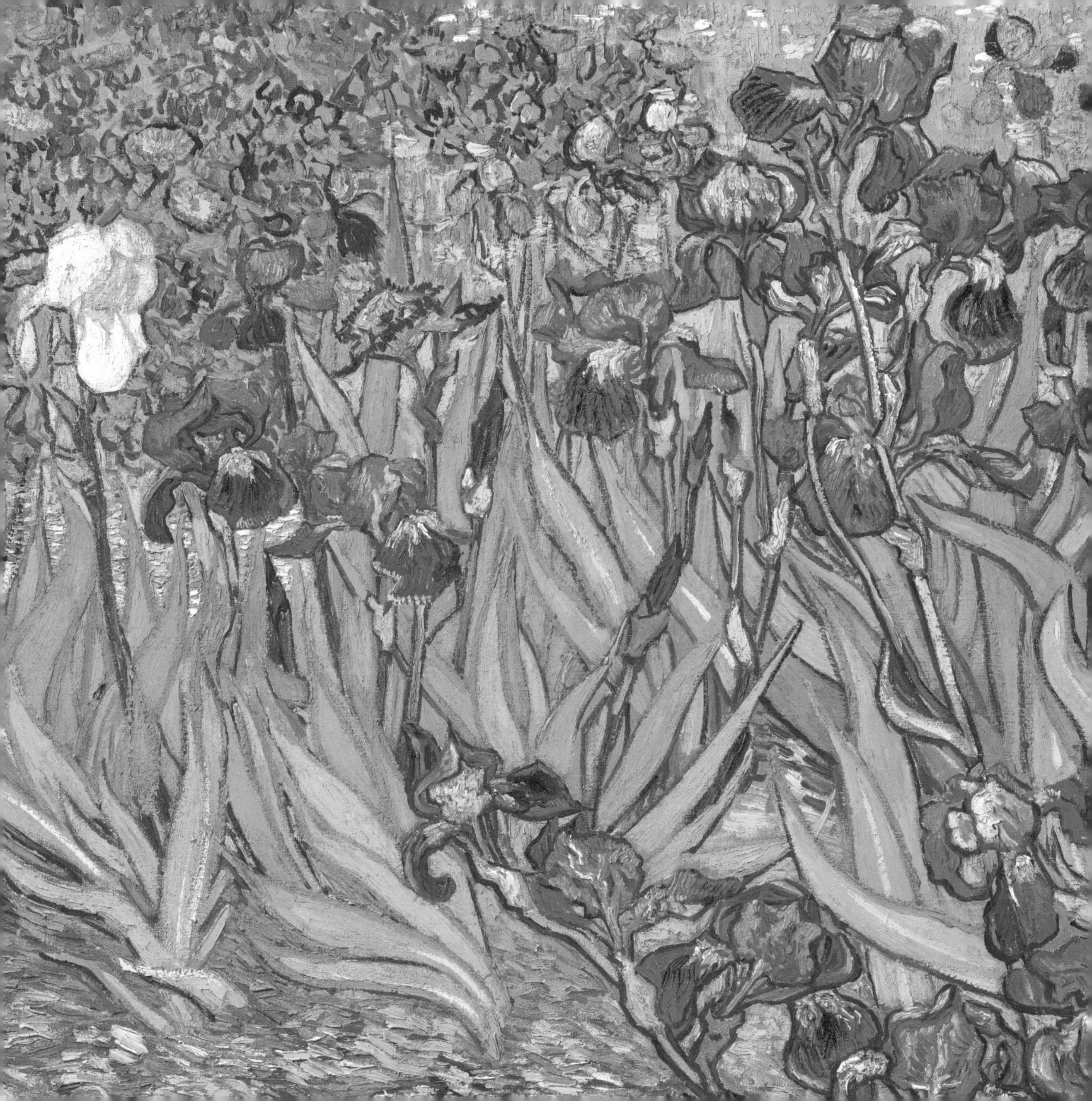

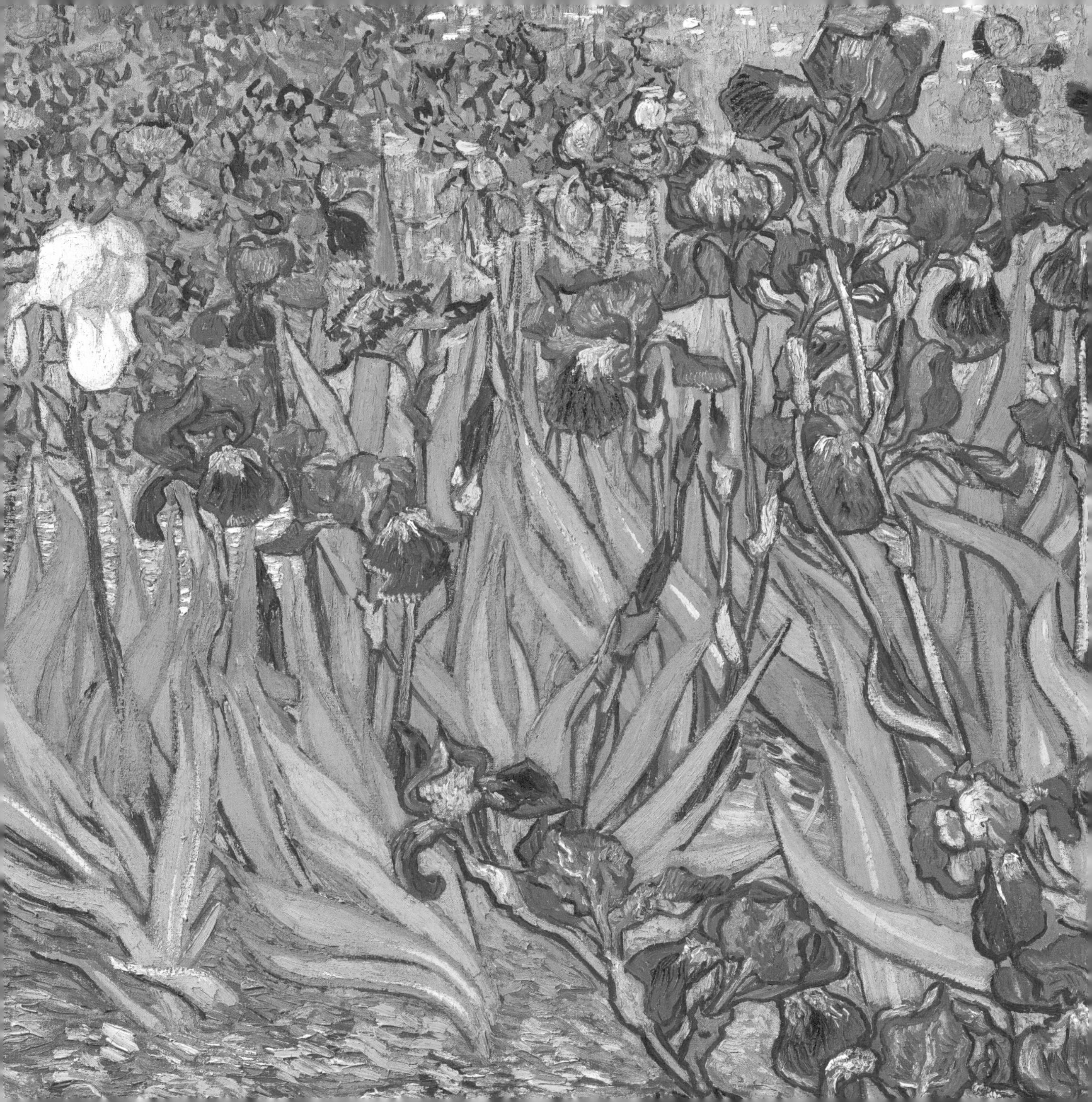

Printed in the USA
CPSIA information can be obtained
at www.ICGtesting.com
LVHW061131121223
766027LV00051B/995